ADDICTIVE

31-Day Devotionals for Life

A Series

Deepak Reju
Series Editor

ADDICTIVE HABITS

CHANGING FOR GOOD

DAVID R. DUNHAM

P&R
PUBLISHING
P.O. BOX 817 • PHILLIPSBURG • NEW JERSEY 08865-0817

Unless otherwise indicated, Scripture quotations are from the ESV Bible® (The Holy Bible, English Standard Version ®), copyright © 2001 by Crossway, a publishing ministry of Good News Publishers. Used by permission. All rights reserved.

Scripture quotations marked (NIV) are from the HOLY BIBLE, NEW INTERNATIONAL VERSION®. NIV®. Copyright © 1973, 1978, 1984 by International Bible Society. Used by permission of Zondervan Publishing House. All rights reserved.

Italics within Scripture quotations indicate emphasis added.

The names of individuals mentioned in this text have been changed to protect their identity. In some cases a composite character has been created.

Printed in the United States of America

Library of Congress Cataloging-in-Publication Data

Names: Dunham, David R., author.
Title: Addictive habits : changing for good / David R. Dunham.
Description: Phillipsburg NJ : P&R Publishing Company, [2018] | Series: 31-day devotionals for life | Includes bibliographical references.
Identifiers: LCCN 2018033673| ISBN 9781629954431 (paperback) | ISBN 9781629954448 (epub) | ISBN 9781629954455 (mobi)
Subjects: LCSH: Addicts--Religious life. | Compulsive behavior--Religious aspects--Christianity. | Devotional exercises.
Classification: LCC BV4596.A24 D86 2018 | DDC 248.8/69--dc23
LC record available at https://lccn.loc.gov/2018033673

To my friend and mentor Frank Tallerico.

Frank not only taught me how to be a counselor
but has counseled me many times over the years.

Without his help and insight,
I would not be who I am today.

Contents

Restructuring

Remaining

Tips for Reading This Devotional

EARLY IN OUR MARRIAGE, my wife and I lived on the top floor of a town house, in a small one-bedroom apartment. Whenever it rained, leaks in the roof would drip through the ceiling and onto our floors. I remember placing buckets in different parts of the apartment and watching the water slowly drip, one drop at a time. I put large buckets out and thought, *It'll take a while to fill them.* The water built up over time, and often I was surprised at how quickly those buckets filled up, overflowing if I didn't pay close enough attention.

This devotional is just like rain filling up a bucket. It's slow, and it builds over time. Just a few verses every day. Drip. Drip. Drip. Just a few drops of Scripture daily to satiate your parched soul.

We start with Scripture. God's Word is powerful. In fact, it's the most powerful force in the entire universe.[1] It turns the hearts of kings, brings comfort to the lowly, and gives spiritual sight to the blind. It transforms lives and turns them upside down. We know that the Bible is God's very own words, so we read and study it to know God himself.

Our study of Scripture is practical. Theology should change how we live. It's crucial to connect the Word with your struggles. Often, as you read this devotional, you'll see the word *you* because David speaks directly to you, the reader. Each reading contains reflection questions and a practical suggestion. You'll get much more from this experience if you answer the questions and do the practical exercises. Don't skip them. Do them for the sake of your own soul.

Our study of Scripture is worshipful. Fundamentally, any addictive habit is a worship problem. We've lost our orientation toward the One who should rule our lives, and we need to turn back to him. The Word points us to Christ, who rescues us from our plight and reorients our life. The goal of your time in God's Word should always be worship. As you grow in your affections for Christ, the King, you put to death your affections for your addiction. The expulsive power of a greater affection for Christ can transform your soul. Adore Christ. Love him. Cherish him. Praise him. Honor him. Give your whole life to him. Don't hold anything back.

If you find this devotional helpful (and I trust that you will!), reread it in different seasons of your life. Work through it this coming month, and then come back to it a year from now, to remind yourself of how to find hope in Christ.

This devotional is *not* meant to be a comprehensive guide to fighting addictions. Good volumes are already written for that purpose. Buy them and make good use of them. You'll see several resources listed at the end of the book.

That's enough for now. Let's begin.

Deepak Reju

Introduction

I NEVER PLANNED to pastor "addicts." As a young pastor fresh out of seminary, I not only had zero experience with substance abuse but also didn't know anyone who had a substance abuse problem. Then God threw me into the deep end of ministry. I found myself as the counseling pastor of a church plant composed mostly of men and women from drug and alcohol rehab. It was the ministry of "God, I don't know what I'm doing!" It was humbling for me, but it also opened my eyes to a serious issue. Over the past eight years, God has given me ever-increasing opportunities to work with those who have a variety of addictive habits: pornography, food, shopping, video games, and substance abuse (to name a few). My burden is to help, and God has been pleased to teach me many things. Some things I want to share with you in this book. Some things God will teach you himself as you walk this difficult journey with him.

Here's what you must believe in order to successfully fight your own addiction: *God has much to say in his Word about addictions.*

Perhaps that surprises you. After all, if you do a word search, you will not find a single reference to the word *addiction* in the Bible. This lack of evidence causes some to dismiss the relevance of the Scriptures to this topic, but the Bible has a lot to say about addictions if you know *how* it speaks about them. You won't find *alcoholic* or *addict* in the Bible, nor will you read about sex addicts, food addicts, gambling addicts, or narcotics abusers. You will read about idolaters and drunkards. The Bible does not use our modern psychological or DSM-approved labels, but it does have its own way of discussing these same issues.

Our modern context has two dominant ways of speaking

about the nature of addiction. It speaks about addiction as being a disease or a choice. Either your addiction is beyond your control and the result of a bad brain, or your addiction is entirely your choice and, to stop, you simply need to choose differently. Of course, the lived experience of addicts tells us something else. It tells us that addictions navigate a unique terrain between voluntarism and sickness. *We are both responsible for our choices and yet enslaved to them.*[1] Sasha does not want to go home and drink a whole bottle of Jim Beam, but she knows that she will. Jeff tries to stop eating after just two Oreos, but once he starts he feels like he can't stop himself.

The Bible acknowledges this reality when it discusses the doctrine of sin. For we are at one and the same time sinners *by choice* and sinners *by birth*. We are both sinners in *action* and sinners in *nature*. If this news sounds hopeless, then you need to remember the rest of the story: *God has a solution for sin!*

My friend Brad has been sober now for fourteen years. When I asked him how he'd done it, his answer was indicative of his character. "Jesus made the difference," he said. Such an answer is what makes Brad a wise counselor to other addicts, but he is not unique. The same answer came from Brandon, as he shared how he'd overcome pornography, and from Sarah, who overcame an eating disorder, and from Cathy, who quit cutting. They all pointed to Jesus.

In the process of fighting their addictive habits, Brad, Brandon, Sarah, and Cathy had done many things to change. They had worked hard, they had turned from sin, they had sought accountability, and they had restructured their lives in order to resist temptation. At the end of the day, though, they all attributed their "recovery" to Jesus. He is the key. The gospel can turn around the life of any addict. Jesus will make the difference in your battle against addictive habits. Whatever your habit, whatever your struggle, Jesus can transform your life. You need Jesus, and that is true even if you are a Christian. As a believer, you will need the constant reminders of the gospel and of God's love for you. That day-to-day reminder of truth keeps us motivated and oriented in the right direction.

Far too many Christians think of the gospel as a message they believed once, at the moment of conversion, before moving on to more important and significant matters. This is especially true when we think about addictive habits. We can easily become so consumed with following steps and adhering to the wisdom of the world that we forget that the power of God brings about change. The gospel is the power of God for salvation (see Rom. 1:16). We need to remember it, meditate on it, be inspired and motivated by it, and live in it. That's what this book is designed to help you do. The thirty-one devotional studies are aimed at reminding you how much you need God's help in order to change and how much God delights to help you change. Each day contains a verse to meditate on, a short lesson to help you reflect on that verse, and a series of questions to help you apply the verse in your life. The more time you spend with God meditating on the gospel, the more empowered you will be for the fight to change your addictive habits.

There is a lot of work ahead of you, friend. I don't want you to be naive about the difficulty of change. Reading this devotional will not grant you victory over sin and addiction in your life. You must seek out others—a godly disciple, a wise pastor, and a biblical counselor—who can walk alongside you and help you to wrestle with your own heart. This book is simply one tool among many that can be a resource for motivating you to change.

As you read, cry out to God for insight and wisdom. James 1:5 tells us that "if any of you lacks wisdom, he should ask God, who gives generously to all" (NIV). Would you ask God to grant you wisdom to know yourself and know him better? You need help, and God delights to give it. Change is possible, because God is in the business of transforming you (see Phil. 1:6).

RESPONSIBILITY

Freedom begins with our willingness to accept our own role in cultivating our addictive habits. While addictions turn into bondage, they always begin with choices. Repenting of sin requires admitting responsibility— we must admit responsibility for our actions, attitudes, thoughts, and desires. This section invites you to meditate on your responsibility as a part of your repentance.

DAY 1

Shame, Identity, and Change

Therefore, if anyone is in Christ, he is a new creation. The old has passed away; behold, the new has come. (2 Cor. 5:17)

WHAT DEFINES YOU MOST? Is it your job, your fears, the opinions of others, or, worst of all, your addiction? Does your addiction shape your identity more than anything else? Addictions never stay at the level of behavior. Instead, they strike at our sense of self. The deeper we go into an addiction, the more we may feel that we *become* it.

Paul Tripp explains: "The longer we struggle with a problem, the more likely we are to define ourselves by that problem (divorced, addicted, depressed, co-dependent, ADD). We come to believe that our problem is who we are. But while these labels may describe particular ways we struggle as sinners in a fallen world, they are not our identity! If we allow them to define us, we will live trapped within their boundaries."[1] Addictions say, "This is who you are, and you'll never change."

Addictions impact our identity in two ways. First, *an addiction requires us to give up significant parts of our life.* We abandon dreams, jobs, family ties, moral convictions, and more. The deeper an addiction goes, the greater the sacrifices become. As a result, significant parts of self are lost in pursuit of addictive habits. Second, *the deeper into an addiction we go, the less willing we are to be vulnerable and open to others.* We fear exposure. Identity is formulated in relationship with others, but the addict misses this key element.

Your addiction defines you. Who you are becomes synonymous with what you do. One evidence of this is the shame you begin to feel, which signals that you have formed your identity

17

around your addiction. You feel shame because you hate yourself. The deeper your experience of shame, the more hopeless you tend to feel about the possibility of change. The result is that you are less willing to fight your addiction.

But there is hope through Christ. Yes, you are a sinner; but in the gospel you are forgiven. In Christ, your identity has been re-formed, so that now you are not a sinner, not an addict, not an alcoholic. *First and foremost, you are a Christian.* Shame is dismantled in Christ, because he gives a new identity. "Therefore, if anyone is in Christ, he is a new creation." You no longer are what you once were. "The old has passed away; behold, the new has come."

Shame says, "I am my addiction." Your emotions tempt you to believe that lie. Christ takes that identity from you and gives you a new one. Your identity is grounded in his victorious work, not in your failure. It is grounded in his triumph over sin, not in your struggle with sin. In him, you may still struggle, but there is hope of freedom because you are not defined by your struggle. You are defined by your relationship to him!

Reflect: How has your addiction influenced your sense of identity? Who do you think you really are? How does the gospel challenge that view of self?

Act: Spend time meditating on the gospel. Read gospel books (such as *A Gospel Primer for Christians* by Milton Vincent), listen to songs, or download sermons that will put the gospel front and center for you this week.

DAY 2

You Can Change Because
God Is Changing You

*Many . . . walk as enemies of the cross of Christ. Their end is
destruction, their god is their belly, and they glory in their shame,
with minds set on earthly things. But our citizenship is in heaven, and
from it we await a Savior, the Lord Jesus Christ, who will transform
our lowly body to be like his glorious body, by the power that enables
him even to subject all things to himself. (Phil. 3:18–21)*

CHANGE REQUIRES BOTH work and surrender. Paul says,
"Work out your own salvation with fear and trembling"—the
Philippians were responsible to fight for their faith (Phil. 2:12).
Yet he adds, "For it is God who works in you, both to will and to
work for his good pleasure" (v. 13). In Scripture we are called to
work because God works in us. In your battle against addictive
habits, you will have to both work and surrender.

This duality is important. If you don't fight sin, you will
never change. You will fail to follow Jesus. Yet, if you think that
all your striving is what produces change, you will drift toward
self-reliance and self-righteousness.

Paul warns in Philippians 3 that we are not to neglect the first
part of this equation: our responsibility. Verses 18 and 19 set up
the warning. There are some who Paul says "walk as enemies of
the cross of Christ." Their lifestyle denies or distorts the gospel of
Jesus. "Their god is their belly"—they are ruled by their desires.
"They glory in their shame"—they delight in immorality. They
set their minds "on earthly things"—they are consumed with
ungodly thoughts. Their end is destruction. It's a warning to all: if
you do not make it your goal to follow Jesus, you will be an enemy
of the cross. Paul warns us to strive after godliness.

Yet Paul reassures us, too. If all our hope hinged on our faithfulness, we would have little reason to hope. We are frail and fickle. Paul gives this encouragement in verses 20–21: Jesus Christ will transform you. While these "enemies" have their minds set on earthly things, Christians have a "citizenship . . . in heaven, and from it we await a Savior." We have every reason to hope, because this Savior is coming. He will transform our weakness, frailty, fickleness, and inconsistency. The same "power that enables him even to subject all things to himself" is the power at work in us. We can trust this Savior because he "[works] in us that which is pleasing" to him (see Heb. 13:21). We have the promise that "he who began a good work in you will bring it to completion at the day of Jesus Christ" (Phil. 1:6). This is a rock-solid guarantee. We labor against our addiction because ultimately God will change us.

God calls you to action—there is no passivity in the Christian life. Yet you have this confidence: the Lord Jesus Christ will transform you! His work is the sure guarantee of your hope; your work is the response of confidence.

Reflect: In what ways do you need to work harder? What things do you need to surrender to God? What does it mean to "surrender" to God?

Act: Write out a prayer confessing your dependence and asking God for specific help with fighting your addiction.

DAY 3

You Become What You Worship

Their idols are silver and gold, the work of human hands. They have mouths, but do not speak; eyes, but do not see. They have ears, but do not hear; noses, but do not smell. They have hands, but do not feel; feet, but do not walk; and they do not make a sound in their throat. Those who make them become like them; so do all who trust in them. (Ps. 115:4–8)

IN SEVERAL PASSAGES in the Old Testament, God uses the language of sensory-organ malfunction to describe the spiritual blindness that is concomitant with idolatry (see Isa. 42:17–20; 43:8–10; 44:9–20).[1] Just as idols have eyes and ears that are carved on them but do not actually work, those who worship such idols lose their spiritual senses. What we worship has the power to conform us to its image. So the psalmist writes, "Those who make them become like them; so do all who trust in them."

We see this happen with Israel's false worship. In Exodus 32, after the people made a golden calf and bowed down to it, God refers to them as stiff-necked (see v. 9). In Hosea 4:16, the false gods were making the Israelites look different from what God had called them to be.

We too become what we worship—only we don't usually worship cattle or little statues. We worship things like money, sex, physical appearance, possessions, control, and respect. Worshipping any of these things will alter us over time. Dillon worshipped money; and, the more he acquired, the more greedy and insecure he became. Amy worshipped the praise of others, and she found herself willing to do things she had sworn she would never do. Anderson worshipped control, and when he wasn't in control he became angry, manipulative, and abusive. Idolatrous worship drove each of these people to false hopes, ungodly behavior, and bad ethics. Who they were was dramatically changed by their worship of false gods.

If we worship our way into the problem of addiction, we must worship our way out, too. The Bible tells us that worshipping Jesus makes us look more like him. As we increasingly behold the "glory of the Lord," we are being transformed into his image "from one degree of glory to another" (2 Cor. 3:18). The goal of the Christian life is to be conformed to the image of the divine Son (see Rom. 8:29). If worship shapes us, then we ought to be increasingly consumed with the worship of the Son.

This truth means that we must take responsibility for our hearts' desires. What do you love about your addictive substance, habit, or person? What do you love about food, porn, drugs, alcohol, or shopping? How do these things draw your heart away from God? How does God offer you a better alternative? How is your pursuit of your addiction really worship? How is it idolatrous? Slow down and wrestle with these questions and, as you admit your false worship, turn to God in repentance. He is ready to receive you again (see 1 John 1:9).

Reflect: Write out your answers to the questions in the last paragraph. Give serious thought to each one.

Act: Make two columns on a sheet of paper. On one side of the page, write out what you love about your addiction. On the other side, write the alternative that God offers to your desires (if you don't know, ask a friend, pastor, or counselor for help).

DAY 4

On Loving and Hating Your Habit

I do not understand my own actions. For I do not do what
I want, but I do the very thing I hate. (Rom. 7:15)

IN THE AFTERMATH of failure, it's usually easy to hate our sins. After you've given in to that piece of chocolate cake, or taken another drink, or succumbed to the temptation to click on that link, feelings of guilt make it easy to hate your addiction. Given enough time, however, you will again be attracted to it. Most of us both love and hate what we do. True change requires us to be honest about the love/hate relationship that we have with our various addictions.

Perhaps to our surprise, the apostle Paul can relate to this tension. Paul writes in Romans 7 about his own struggle with the flesh—his tension between the desire to obey God and the desire to sin. He has the "desire to do what is right" (v. 18), but when he goes to do what is right there is another desire at work in him. He doesn't do the good that he wants to do, he says, but instead he does what he hates (see v. 15). Paul knows what it is to be double-minded about his sin.

Double-minded is a good descriptor of how we often feel about our sin. We hate it and want to change; but when we make efforts to do just that, we find that we still love our sin and don't want to give it up. Can you see your own double-mindedness at work with your addictive habit? Maybe you hate your impulsive buying, but when it comes time to cut up your credit card you have second thoughts. Maybe you hate pornography, but when you feel convicted to lock down your smartphone you hesitate. Maybe you're reluctant to confess your sin. After all, once it's out there, you are inviting accountability—and you're not ready to change.

23

God knows your internal struggles. He understands your love/hate relationship with your sins and addictive habits. It is important to be candid about this tension. If you pretend that you perfectly hate your sin, you will not be prepared for the hard fight that awaits you. There is something you love about your habit. What is it? When you hate your sin, what do you hate about it? Identify this tension so that you can be prepared to fight hard against temptation.

Paul knows the hold that our sin has on us, but he also knows the One who can free us from it. "Who can free me from this body of sin?" he cries out. His answer is Jesus! You most likely have a love/hate relationship with your sin. Be honest about that relationship—for only then will you be inclined, like Paul, to cry out to Jesus for rescue.

Reflect: When do you most hate your sin? When do you most love it?

Act: Be on the defense against self-confidence—pride goes before a fall. Memorize Romans 7:24–25a as a way to remind yourself to depend on Jesus for change.

DAY 5

Changing Kingdoms

He has delivered us from the domain of darkness and transferred
us to the kingdom of his beloved Son. (Col. 1:13)

IT WAS THAT great theologian Bob Dylan who said that you
"gotta serve somebody"—whether that somebody is God or the
devil.[1] Every addiction comes with kingdom allegiances. We
indulge in addictive habits because we've committed ourselves to
certain visions of the good life and, as a result, will serve whatever
master most enables those visions to become realities. *Addictions
are about kingdom loyalty.*

The Bible divides the world into two kingdoms: the kingdom
of darkness and the kingdom of Jesus (see Col. 1:13). This harks
back to the Exodus. The Exodus, after all, was the actual, literal,
transfer of God's people from one kingdom (Egypt) to another
kingdom (Israel). What was literal in Exodus becomes a paradigm
for thinking about our own relationship with God. Spiritually
speaking, we are all in a kingdom. There's no neutral territory—
no spiritual Switzerland. We are aligned with either God or the
devil, and to serve the one is to necessarily hate the other (see
Matt. 6:24). Every time you and I decide to indulge our addictive
habits, we set ourselves against God. Our allegiances are not to
the Lord; instead, we choose the kingdom of darkness.

Yet the nature of an addiction is such that indulging doesn't
always feel like our choice. Taking that drink, buying that blouse,
clicking that link, or entertaining that thought can sometimes feel
beyond our control. In Colossians 1:13, Paul does not present the
solution to your addiction as a decision to stop serving the kingdom of darkness and to serve God instead. That's the way some
people treat addictions, and maybe that's how some people have

spoken to you about your addictive habit. Maybe you've even thought that way yourself. *I can do this on my own. I can fix the problem. I just say no to sin and choose to follow God.* To be sure, our choices are vitally important. Joshua challenged the people of Israel, and us, to "choose this day whom you will serve" (Josh. 24:15). But Paul recognizes that we need to be delivered. The transfer from one kingdom to another comes from Jesus.

There's that duality at work again. Changing kingdoms requires us to desire to follow God, yet the actual transfer must come by means of Jesus Christ. You need rescuing! Jesus can save you. He can move you from the kingdom of darkness to his very own kingdom.

Often I meet guys in recovery programs who tell me that they need to make it on their own. "I have to do this for myself, by myself," they say. Of course, they do need to decide to quit and get sober—their choice is not irrelevant. But most have already tried to help themselves in the past, and to no avail. There must be a real rescue—a savior who comes to their aid.

What's true for their struggle is true for yours, regardless of your addictive habit. You must be delivered. As you fight to change your kingdom allegiance, ask Christ to deliver you. In fact, ask him right now.

> **Reflect:** How do your addictive habits reveal an allegiance to a kingdom of darkness? How have you tried and failed to change on your own?
>
> **Act:** God calls us to be active participants in our change, but there are some things that only God can do. Make a list of the things that you know you are responsible to do and a list of the things that only God can do.

DAY 6

Check Your Loves

But each person is tempted when he is lured and enticed by his own desire. Then desire when it has conceived gives birth to sin, and sin when it is fully grown brings forth death. (James 1:14–15)

HAVE YOU NOTICED that everything is somebody else's fault? "He/she made me do it." "The devil made me do it." Or perhaps the cause of our sins and failures lies in our circumstances: "If I had a better job, a better car, a better spouse, or better parents, then I wouldn't do what I do." In truth, however, the Bible teaches us that the root of our problems is our own hearts. James teaches us that *what we desire can lead us to sin.*

Often we think that the lure that catches us is external. Like a fish seeing a line dropped into the water, we are tempted to take a bite of the bait that catches our eye. We see something desirable, and we are tricked into chomping down on the hook hidden behind it. But James says that we are lured and enticed by our own desire. What we love drives what we do. Temptation arises first from our own internal desires. You simply cannot tell yourself to stay out of the cookie jar. You're hungry. Your love of chocolate will tempt you to eat, sometimes until you're sick. *Desire drives what we do.*

James describes a straightforward progression toward sin. It starts with a desire that entices us to act on our passions. Once we act, the desire conceives and gives birth to sin. As we indulge in that sin, it grows; and as it grows, it brings forth its own result: death. Desires can be dangerous. They start simply, with an interest, and end in destruction.

What you desire will drive what you do—but *what you desire is always deeper than your addictive habit.* Billy, for example, didn't

27

love spending money. He loved the comfort of new things, and when he was feeling depressed he would buy a lot of them (pickup trucks, tools, computers, televisions, and so on). He didn't love spending, nor did he really love things—what he loved was the momentary pleasure that new things gave him. He loved the feeling of getting some new toy. Sally, likewise, didn't love alcohol. In fact, she would have told you that she hated alcohol—but what she loved was the feeling of numbness. When she was sober, she heard every negative and condemning comment that people had ever said about her. She heard all those voices in her head, again and again and again. When she was drunk, though, she didn't hear them anymore. She loved the quiet.

What do you love? Think beneath the surface of your addictive habit. How do your desires drive what you do? This is the question that you need to wrestle with, and you should wrestle hard. There are no innocent desires when it comes to sin. Do war against your passions, for what you desire will lure and entice you to sin—and sin, when it is fully grown, will bring forth death. Don't let your desires for the wrong things ruin your life.

Reflect: What desires might lie beneath or behind your addictive habit? What "death" has been produced in your life as a result of these desires?

Act: Ultimately, *sinful* desires are *selfish* desires. Strategize about how you might turn your selfish desire into an opportunity to serve others. Then put your plan into action.

DAY 7

Graves of Craving

"The LORD heard you when you wailed, 'If only we had meat to eat! We were better off in Egypt!' Now the LORD will give you meat, and you will eat it . . . until it comes out of your nostrils and you loathe it—because you have rejected the LORD, who is among you, and have wailed before him." (Num. 11:18, 20 NIV)

HUNGER CAN BE a powerful driving force. We've invented the word *hangry* to describe that feeling of irritation we get when we haven't eaten for a while. But bodily cravings are not just about biological need. Our cravings can lead to sinful desires and attitudes. Thus, our cravings should not be blindly obeyed.

We can appreciate Israel's concerns in this passage. Here they were, a massive people group, wandering in the wilderness with no guaranteed food. As they reflect on this need, they grumble and complain. God speaks of Israel as having "rejected the LORD" (v. 20). Their cravings lead them away from God. In fact the text describes a rather grotesque scene in which their cravings became a sort of addiction.

God declares that if Israel wants food they will get it. They will eat—but they will eat until they are stuffed and the taste of the food becomes loathsome. They will eat even though they no longer want to; they will become so full of meat that it oozes out of their nostrils (see v. 20). They will continue to eat even though eating will ultimately kill them. They even call the land where all of this takes place Kibroth-hattaavah, which means "graves of craving" (v. 34).[1] They indulge despite the negative consequences, despite their eventual death, and they can't stop even though they want to stop. This is the epitome of an addiction.

The key to this passage is to understand the power of their

cravings. A desire for food is understandable—natural, even. But this was more than just biology at work. Their cravings became excessive, obsessive, and idolatrous. They wanted more than they needed (until it came out of their nostrils), and in ways that they didn't need it (through a desire to return to Egypt). Not every cry of the body is legitimate.

You don't have to obey your bodily cravings—especially ones that morph into sinful attitudes and actions rather than remaining mere biological need. Remind yourself of this truth, and be sensitive to the distinction between biology and idolatry. Don't assume that because your body is crying out for something, you actually need it. Your cravings may lead to death. Be honest about what is desire and what is need.

Reflect: Think about your addictive cravings. What is your biological need? When does that biology escalate into idolatry? Can you distinguish between the two: biology and excessive, obsessive, idolatrous desire?

Act: Learn to tell yourself no to small desires as you try to fight against these bigger addictive habits. Tell yourself no to four simple things each day this week—for example, say no to an extra cookie or to one more episode of a show on Netflix.

DAY 8

Check Your Attitude

*Finally, brothers, whatever is true, whatever is honorable,
whatever is just, whatever is pure, whatever is lovely, whatever
is commendable, if there is any excellence, if there is anything
worthy of praise, think about these things. (Phil. 4:8)*

"WHAT'S THE POINT?" Kevin exclaimed. He had reached a
point in our counseling where he was hopeless and discouraged.
Kevin often lived with a sense of defeat. It became clear to me
that part of his struggle was related to his attitude. As long as he
was convinced that there was no point in fighting, he wouldn't
fight. Despair will always win when we don't take charge of our
thoughts.

What we dwell on in our minds has incredible power. If we
view life through our own biased, negative lens, we will inevi-
tably find fault in everything. If we dwell on failure, we will
become convinced that we can never succeed. If we dwell on
self-condemnation, we will convince ourselves that we are condemned by everyone—perhaps even God. What we dwell on is
powerful, and the attitudes that result from our thought life can
shape our efforts at change.

In this passage, Paul is addressing the issue of anxiety. Anxiety can easily lead to despair, and so Paul gives the Philippians a
challenge. "Think on these things," he says. To fight back against
anxious thoughts, Paul invites meditation on more commendable
things. *Thinking becomes a powerful tool for fighting for change.* The
Greek word used here for *think* may mean to "calculate," "evalu-
ate," or "consider." Some translations say "dwell on." Change
does not come simply from mentally assenting to "these things."
It comes from serious, deep meditation and reflection on these

commendable qualities. We need to wrestle with what is "true" and calculate in our minds whatever things are "lovely."

Dwelling on "these things" means moving them from abstraction to specifics. Certainly we should focus on these things as they apply to life in general. It's easy to focus on everything wrong in life and to miss all the lovely and excellent things. But ultimately the point of the passage is to fix our minds on that which is the epitome of all these things: Jesus. Each of these items finds its ultimate expression in Jesus.

So who is true? Jesus (see John 1:17; 14:6). Who is honorable? Jesus (see John 5:23). Who is just? Jesus (see Rev. 15:3). Who is pure? Jesus (see 1 John 3:3). Who is lovely? Jesus (see Ps. 45:2). Who is commendable? Jesus (see Rev. 5:12). Who is excellent? Jesus (see Heb. 1:4). Who is worthy of praise? Jesus (see Heb. 3:3; Rev. 4:11; 5:9, 12). We must fix our minds on Jesus; he is the true realization of all these qualities.

Take responsibility for your attitude. What you dwell on will shape you and influence your efforts at change. Dwell on Jesus. Fix your mind to him and find that change is possible.

Reflect: What do you believe about change? Like Kevin, do you believe there is no point in fighting? Where does your mind most often go when confronted with difficulty? Do you condemn yourself? Do you despair? Do you feel like a failure? Are you hard on yourself?

Act: Make a list describing how Jesus reflects each of the eight qualities listed in Philippians 4:8. Then meditate and pray through this list. Start cultivating a new habit of focusing your mind on Jesus.

DAY 9

Don't Romanticize Your Addiction

And the whole congregation of the people of Israel grumbled against Moses and Aaron in the wilderness, . . . "Would that we had died by the hand of the LORD in the land of Egypt, when we sat by the meat pots and ate bread to the full, for you have brought us out into this wilderness to kill this whole assembly with hunger." (Ex. 16:2–3)

WHAT WAS ISRAEL THINKING? Their recall of life in Egypt was highly skewed. They remembered lots of food but forgot that it came with chains. It was the equivalent of saying, "Sure, the Egyptians tried to kill our babies; but, man, did they have good bread." That's absurd. Yet their skewed perspective is not all that different from our own thinking. *If you romanticize your addiction, you will always be tempted to run back to it.*

Life outside Egypt was hard, to be sure. The Israelites were marching to freedom, but crossing the wilderness was no stroll in the park. It came with hardship and required trust in the Lord, which is exactly how God designed it. Here's the problem—as Israel wrestled with all these struggles, they kept looking over their shoulders. They cast an eye back to the comforts of food that had come with Egyptian bondage.

We are no different than the Israelites. We are often ready for freedom, but when we realize that freedom comes with a cumbersome journey, we become reluctant to leave our own slavery. Addictive habits bring a sense of comfort. Buying a new purse can relieve some temporary discouragement. Eating a carton of ice cream can feel like spending time with an old friend when we are lonely. Alcohol can wash away the guilt of unresolved conflict. *There are hundreds of ways that our addictions provide us comfort, but we can so romanticize those comforts that we gloss over the destruction they produce.*

Shopping, eating, and drinking don't fix our problems. Such indulgences only temporarily distract us from them. When we come down from our "high," we still have issues to resolve. And, sadly, our addictive habits will likely have added to the mess. Each vice comes with its own unique physical, financial, relational, and spiritual consequences. Our addictive habits compound the messes that they try to avoid.

What did the Israelites need in order to persevere in the wilderness? Honesty about the trials of Egypt and the God who had freed them. When you romanticize your addictive habit, you will be tempted to return to it—or perhaps never to leave it at all. When you can be honest about its destructiveness and candid about the nature of the God who wants to free you, then there is hope.

Reflect: Be honest—how do you romanticize your sin?

Act: Write out a "break-up" letter to your addictive habit. Explain everything that is wrong with it and why you must part ways. Share it with a friend who can remind you of truth when you are tempted to romanticize.

RELATIONSHIP

True and lasting change that counts doesn't happen simply through behavioral modification. Change is intimately related to the person and work of Jesus Christ in your life and to your involvement with his church. This section will invite you to meditate on the character of God and on your relationship with Jesus and with others.

DAY 10

Who Is God?

*"The LORD, the LORD, a God merciful and gracious, slow to anger,
and abounding in steadfast love and faithfulness, keeping steadfast
love for thousands, forgiving iniquity and transgression and sin,
but who will by no means clear the guilty." (Ex. 34:6–7)*

"NOBODY SAW ME." That was Jeremy's defense when I confronted him about looking at porn at the campus library. His Christian witness was intact, he maintained. Of course, the reality was that the Lord had seen him, and Jeremy ought to have held God in higher regard. How you think about God dramatically impacts how you deal with sin.

God tells us who he is. We do not have the right to think of God differently from how he has revealed himself to be. So we need to pay careful attention to how God speaks of himself: as merciful and just.

The first portion of God's description of himself to Moses (vv. 6–7a) emphasizes his mercy and grace. "Steadfast love" refers to his enduring love for those who commit "iniquity and transgression and sin." Addictions draw us away from God, but he invites us back. He offers love and forgiveness to us.

The second part (v. 7b) points to God's divine justice. He will "by no means clear the guilty." God takes sin seriously, and as a result so should we. He judges sinners and punishes iniquity. Addictions are not simply bad habits; they are distortions of God's will and desires for us. Addictive habits are rebellion against the Lord of the universe, and we ought to fear the consequences—not just on earth but in our relationship with God.

Both God's love and God's justice are vital for us to remember. We cannot emphasize the Lord's love at the expense of his justice or his justice at the expense of his love. If we embrace God's justice without regard for his love, *we will run from him*, attempting to hide from his piercing gaze (see Heb. 4:13). Or, if fear does not strike us, we will respond with hatred. We will see God's justice in relation to our own weakness and will begrudge it. We will become bitter and resentful toward God. But, if we acknowledge God's love with no thought for his justice, *we will see our sin as a small thing*. Not only will we not fear, but we won't regard God at all. We will neglect repentance and reconciliation and will see God's love as tolerance—as though he simply overlooks our sin.

We need a view of God that includes both his justice and his love. How you respond after you sin reveals what you really think about God. Addictive habits will convince us either that God can't love us or that he doesn't care. Both responses are wrong. God tells us what he is like; we need to submit to his self-revelation in his Word.

Reflect: What do you think of when you think of God? Do you struggle with remembering his love or his justice?

Act: Read and pray through these verses on God's love: Ps. 86:15; John 3:16; Rom. 5:8; 8:37–39; Eph. 2:4–5; and on his justice: 2 Chron. 19:7; Job 34:12; Ps. 9:7–8; Isa. 61:8; 2 Thess. 1:8–9.

DAY 11

Jesus, Friend of Sinners

And the Pharisees and the scribes grumbled, saying, "This
man receives sinners and eats with them." (Luke 15:2)

THE RELIGIOUS LEADERS of Jesus's day separated themselves from sinners. They had a long-standing conviction that
association with certain kinds of people meant contamination.
The fact, then, that Jesus ate with, stayed with, and attracted sinners made a distinction in their minds: *Jesus is not one of us.* Jesus
was different; he *loved* and *welcomed* all sinners.

Think about how we treat other people's sin. Certain sins are
excused. If you're a glutton, no big deal—there is room for you at
the church potluck. Other sins are condemned. If you're a heroin
addict, you may not be welcomed. Jesus knows no such distinction. He spent time with social pariahs, prostitutes, and political
traitors. He touched the diseased and allowed the outcasts to
touch him. All sinners are welcome in Jesus's company—even
those whom society deems the worst.

Jesus ate with sinners. Dining with someone is a significant
act, which has often, throughout history and around the world,
represented acceptance and friendship. Meals put you in close
quarters with someone. Your hands reach into the same dishes.
You talk together. You sit with each other. It is a clear act of wel-
coming, accepting, and befriending. The Pharisees refused to
dine with social pariahs, but that was the precise thing that a
social outcast wanted: community. Jesus provided community
when he ate with sinners. It was an opportunity for him to say,
"You are welcomed and loved." Pariahs are not pariahs in Jesus's
circle; they are friends.

God eats with sinners. That is the overall testimony of the

Scriptures (see Ex. 24:9–11; Lev. 3; Luke 7:36–50; 15:2; 19:1–10). What is true of Jesus's earthly meals with social outcasts is true of the spiritual meal he will share with us. You are a rebel and an outcast, but Jesus died for you so that you can know his acceptance and love. "You who once were far off have been brought near," the apostle Paul says (Eph. 2:13). If you give your life to Christ, you become a part of his family, the church. God welcomes sinners, and Jesus's earthly dining habits reveal this spiritual truth: *he welcomes us to his table to eat the bread of life.* And one day all God's children will recline at the table of the Lord in the kingdom of heaven (see Matt. 8:11), at the greatest banquet of all time (see Rev. 19:6–9). What a glorious day that will be!

Your sin, your addiction, does not disqualify you from an intimate relationship with Jesus. He is a friend of sinners. In fact, the sole reason that he came to earth was to rescue sinners, not to encourage the righteous (see Mark 2:17). Whatever others have said about your sin, whatever you have said about it, Jesus welcomes sinners. He welcomes you. Jesus is a friend of sinners, and your addictive habit should not keep you from him. He invites sinners to himself. Your struggle should drive you *to* Jesus, not *away from* him. Jesus is for sinners.

Reflect: You are invited to a meal with Jesus, who loves, accepts, and welcomes sinners like you and me.

Reflect: Do you struggle to believe that Jesus can be your friend? If so, why? What would it mean for Jesus to be your friend?

Act: Read Mark 2:1–3:6 and list all the ways that Jesus demonstrates his controversial friendship with sinners.

DAY 12

Do You Have Faith?

For this reason I bow my knees before the Father ... that according to the riches of his glory he may grant you to be strengthened with power through his Spirit in your inner being, so that Christ may dwell in your hearts through faith—that you, being rooted and grounded in love, may have strength to comprehend with all the saints what is the breadth and length and height and depth, and to know the love of Christ that surpasses knowledge, that you may be filled with all the fullness of God. (Eph. 3:14, 16–19)

IF YOU'VE TRIED to give up the false loves that lead to your addictive habit, you already know that change is hard. It can be so hard, in fact, that we often feel as if we will never make progress. The key to persevering is to have faith that *God can change you.*

Paul's prayer for the Ephesians could be called his Prayer for Spiritual Strength. He knows that in order to be spiritually strong we must be empowered by God himself. The strength to change is not in us. Change is possible because God is in us. In Ephesians 2, Paul articulates the identity of the believer as the dwelling place of God (see v. 22). In Ephesians 3, he says that God's Spirit is in you (see v. 16). Because we have God dwelling in us, we have the hope to grow and change. His power is at work in us (see Eph. 3:20).

Paul's prayer asks God to strengthen "with power" the "inner being," so that believers will be rooted in, grounded in, and knowledgeable of the love of God. Knowing God's love for us provides hope. It helps us to believe that he can do "far more abundantly than all that we ask" (Eph. 3:20). God's love prompts us to believe that he will change us and that his power is at work within us. The question you must wrestle with is whether you have faith in this God.

41

Do you believe that God loves you? Do you believe that he is at work in you? When you are discouraged by your progress, what do you focus on? Faith prompts you to believe that God is at work even when you don't feel it or see it. It prompts you to believe that God's love is longer, higher, and deeper than your sin. It prompts you to "know the love of Christ that surpasses knowledge" (Eph. 3:19)—that is, to know Christ's love beyond the things we can see and understand. Faith is, as the author to the Hebrews says, "the assurance of things hoped for, the conviction of things not seen" (Heb. 11:1). Faith believes even in the face of reasons to be skeptical.

Change is hard. But, even when it feels impossible, will you trust that God is at work? God *is* at work in you through his Spirit. Have no doubt about that.

What is your part in this fight? Your faith. It is the key to persevering in your fight to change your addictive habits.

Reflect: When you are most tempted to believe that you will never change, what are you focused on?

Act: Make a list of specific ways that you know God is changing you. Add to it as you continue to fight.

DAY 13

Whom Do You Serve?

Live as people who are free, not using your freedom as a cover-up for evil, but living as servants of God (1 Peter 2:16)

FREEDOM. It's a powerful word, though it can feel like an elusive dream to many who struggle with addiction. Addictions are tantamount to bondage—to selfish desires, lies and self-justifications, unrelenting bad habits, self-condemnation, and much more. The world says that freedom comes through self-driven autonomy: "Break free! Run from your addiction! You can overcome this!" But biblical freedom is found not in *autonomy* but in *slavery* to Christ.

This might sound counterintuitive to you. Slavery has lots of negative connotations. But bear with me. The Bible presents men and women as perpetual slaves (see Rom. 6:15–22). We are either slaves to sin or slaves to God. God, in his mercy, has set you free from sin to become a slave to him (see Rom. 6:17–18, 22). Freedom is found in turning from sin and surrendering your life to Christ—and, in that, you become truly free. You become all that God meant you to be. So, to the Christian, freedom is not complete autonomy but slavery to God.

It was typical for believers to think of themselves as slaves to Christ. Peter, Paul, and James all identified themselves as such (see 2 Peter 1:1; Rom. 1:1; James 1:1). When Peter writes about freedom, he parallels it with service to God. To "live as people who are free," in the biblical worldview, is to live as a "servant of God."

Gaining victory over your addiction is not about gaining independence and autonomy. It's tempting to become resentful of all the help that is required for you to overcome an addictive habit.

43

Alonzo was frustrated with the amount of accountability that was required to help him fight his pornography habit. He became recalcitrant, defensive, and stubborn when people checked in on him. He saw overcoming his addiction as the means to getting everyone off his back. The Bible, however, understands freedom differently. Freedom is rooted in our relationship with God. Freedom is slavery to God. We can't find true freedom apart from him.

Think of an addiction as slavery to a habit. We serve our habit in countless ways throughout our addiction. We serve it every time we give in to temptation, or whenever we protect the habit by misleading others about it. We serve it every time we pretend to quit our habit but are actually just attempting to tame it. This is not freedom. It's slavery to your addiction. You are ultimately serving yourself. Self-driven autonomy or independence won't work; it will only perpetuate the problem. When you think of your freedom as devotion and service to God, then you can truly begin to fight back against your habits. As you orient your life around him, he will give you the strength to put to death your addictive habits.

True freedom is found in service to God. Whom are you serving?

Reflect: Slavery to Christ is true freedom. It's better than your self-driven autonomy.

Reflect: When you think about freedom, what comes to your mind? How can you reorder your thinking around biblical freedom—full surrender to Christ? How can you live increasingly in his service?

Act: Find a ministry that you can get involved in at your local church. Begin to fight for freedom by serving God. What ministry will you be a part of? Share this with a friend or counselor.

DAY 14

It's Not about You

So, whether you eat or drink, or whatever you do,
do all to the glory of God. (1 Cor. 10:31)

YOU PICKED THIS book up for a reason. What motivates your desire to change? Not all motives are equally sufficient. In fact, any motive that doesn't begin with God will eventually give out when change becomes hard. Our primary motive for change should be the glory of God.

We often think that our addictive habits will make life easier. In a sense, this is true. Emily played video games constantly in order to suppress stress. The more she played, the less she reflected on how much work she hadn't completed. Of course, over time, all her video game playing meant that more and more work went unfinished. The problems mounted over time. Are you like Emily?

As our problems pile up, life becomes more and more unmanageable. At that moment, we begin to contemplate change. The chaos of life can become motivation for us to turn from our sin. But this motivation will rarely be sufficient for cultivating *lasting* change.

If my motivation stems from the chaos in my life (the difficulty of functioning, the brokenness of my relationships, or the personal pain that I feel), I am unlikely to endure when change becomes hard. Change comes with its own challenges: Life can become more complicated as I give up my addiction. Relational brokenness can be more pronounced. Personal pain arises, especially if biological withdrawal accompanies my change. So what will keep me motivated when all these things happen? Not myself. Not my own strength. Not my ingenuity. The thing that keeps me going is the glory of God.

Paul tells the Corinthians that everything in their lives is to be done for the glory of God. He picks, interestingly, two rather mundane things: eating and drinking. These are normal, universal, everyday activities. We eat and drink without even thinking much about it. Paul's use of these two activities is not random. He selects routine activities in order to highlight the broadness of his next statement: "whatever you do." If these everyday behaviors are to be done for God's glory, then the "whatever" of his next statement is truly expansive. *There is nothing so mundane, so routine, so common, or so necessary that it is beneath the purpose of glorifying God. Everything that we do is for his glory. This includes fighting addictive habits.*

Can you make God's glory your motivation for change? This empowers endurance by bringing to us a *profound* goal. Don't settle for *lesser* goals. If your only reason to quit your addiction is that you are hurting yourself or hurting society, you are stuck. What do you do if both self and society fail to offer any real hope or joy? The glory of God is a bigger, better reason to change. It holds meaning beyond your difficult experiences in this life.

What's your motivation? Is it God, or is it something much less?

Reflect: God's glory is motivation that can get you through hard times.

Reflect: This is not just an intellectual, abstract idea. Practically, what might it look like to glorify God as you fight your addiction?

Act: Write out a commitment statement, at least one paragraph long, that clarifies God's glory as the ultimate goal of your fight against addiction. Pray and ask God to make this a major motivation in your battle against your addictive habit.

DAY 15

Your Spiritual Enemy

Be strong in the Lord and in the strength of his might. . . . For we
do not wrestle against flesh and blood, but against . . . the spiritual
forces of evil in the heavenly places. Therefore take up the whole
armor of God, that you may be able to withstand in the evil day,
and having done all, to stand firm. (Eph. 6:10, 12–13)

ALL AROUND US rages a spiritual war, and our struggles with addictive habits are part of that war. Your fight is far more spiritual than you realize. The apostle Paul helps us in this passage, giving us three key insights about the nature of spiritual warfare.

The devil has schemes (v. 11). The devil attacks believers. He does this primarily in two ways: temptation and accusation. In temptation, he convinces us that what we want he can provide. In these moments, he hides the holiness of God from us, telling us as he told Eve, "God won't really care if you disobey." At other times, Satan *accuses us.* He uses this tactic to hide the love of God from us. He reminds us of our sin, tells us that we can't be forgiven and can't change, and leaves us defeated and discouraged. Both tactics are highly effective and work in tandem. But both schemes are lies, and we need to spot them when Satan throws fiery darts at us.

We wrestle (v. 12). You have relational struggles. You can't stay away from the alcohol, cocaine, or food. You have a hard time resisting your addictive habit. You might hurt yourself or lose your job or disappoint your friends. All of this entails doing battle with "flesh and blood" (v. 12). But Paul's point is that this is not the only battle—or even the most important battle. Remember, you are in the midst of spiritual warfare, battling not just flesh and blood but cosmic powers and spiritual forces of evil. God and Satan stand against each other and at war with each other, and you are smack-dab in the middle of it all. You're part of a much greater war going on around you.

We have God on our side (v. 13). Don't despair. Paul tells us that we do not fight alone. We fight, and can even stand firm, if we put on the full armor of God. Truth, righteousness, the gospel, faith, salvation, Scripture, and prayer—these are the elements of our armor (see vv. 14–18). This is how we defend ourselves against Satan's attack. Satan tempts us to believe lies, so we preach truth to ourselves. He tempts us to substitute our own righteousness for Christ's, so we meditate on the gospel. The devil tempts us to disbelieve God; we cling to faith. The devil seeks to distract us from evangelism and prayer, so we are actively involved in these disciplines. Most importantly, we fight against Satan by knowing God's Word well.

Reflect: Satan conspires against you, but God is for you. As the apostle Paul says, "If God is for us, who can be against us?" (Rom. 8:31).

Reflect: Do you see your struggle as a *spiritual* battle? Or have you reduced your fight to merely "flesh and blood?" Do you see that there is a much greater war going on and that you are a soldier in this battle?

Act: Looking over the list of elements of the armor of God, which do you feel is lacking most in your life? Strategize a way to prepare yourself for spiritual warfare.

The Company You Keep

Do not be deceived: "Bad company ruins good morals." (1 Cor. 15:33)

CALVIN HAD MADE tremendous progress. He was clean and sober, and had been for several months. Then he invited two alcoholics to move in with him. He wanted to be helpful and generous, but there were serious consequences. The company we keep either helps us to fight or tempts us to return to our addictive habits.

Addictions have a social component. Perhaps you started using drugs because your friends did. Or maybe you started overeating because your parents used food as a reward. Or perhaps you started shopping in order to escape a longing for relational intimacy. Our relationships affect us. Granted, relationships don't determine whether we will become addicted—that's a more complicated development. But they do influence our addictions.

Change, too, has a social component. For many years, the recovery culture has highlighted how socialization is vital for change. Individual participants in various programs are often assigned sponsors or mentors to help them stay the course. Change happens best when others help us.

We must be wise and discerning about the company we keep. Paul warns the Corinthians of this principle of association. Throughout his letter, he notes the bad living and bad doctrine of some who are among the Corinthian church. Some even say, "Let us eat and drink, for tomorrow we die" (1 Cor. 15:32). These bad influencers claim that there are no eternal consequences, so we may as well indulge in hedonism.

Do your friends sound like this? Do your parents encourage your indulgences? Do you gravitate toward those who affirm your addictive habits, or who at least turn a blind eye?

Elsewhere in 1 Corinthians, Paul warns us again. Those who we allow to influence our lives can tempt us to ruin. In fact, Paul is so concerned about the influence of immorality in the church that he insists the church remove the sinning man from among them (see 1 Cor. 5:6–11).

Calvin's association with other addicts became a source of temptation. The more time he spent with them, the more he justified his indulgences. Their arguments became his arguments, their lies his lies, their habits his habits. They didn't make him drink; the ultimate choice was his. But their addiction became a point of temptation that undercut his commitment to sobriety. His friends became a liability. They corrupted his life.

Consider your relationships. Who has influence in your life? Do they help you to fight your addictive habits? Or do they enable them? Do they encourage your indulgence in sin? How so? Slow down and take a moment to honestly answer these questions. Don't rush past them.

Addictions have a social component, but so does change. The company that you keep can help you or hurt you. So choose your friends carefully.

Reflect: Your friendships can make or break your addiction. Choose wisely.

Reflect: Who do you need to either cut out of your life—at least for a season—or limit your interaction with? If you are not sure, pray and ask God for discernment.

Act: Ask a wise, mature friend, parent, counselor, or pastor to connect you with people who can help you to grow in faith and fight your addiction.

DAY 17

A Burden to Bear

Bear one another's burdens, and so fulfill the law of Christ. (Gal. 6:2)

CHANGE REQUIRES helping hands. When we struggle, we are often tempted to pull inward—to create distance and space between ourselves and others. Sometimes we do this out of fear of judgment or embarrassment. Other times we do it because we fear burdening others. But if we want to change, we don't have the luxury of hiding our burdens. *Helping hands increase our likelihood of finding lasting change.*

"The law of Christ" is a peculiar phrase. What does it mean? It references Jesus's response to the Pharisees' question about the greatest commandment. When asked about the greatest commandment, Jesus said it was to love God and love others (see Mark 12:28–31). The law of Christ means, in part, to love one another.

Love is demonstrated when we bear each other's burdens. In Galatians 6:1, Paul talks about those who are "caught in any transgression"—that is, they are mired in some kind of sin struggle. Those who are "caught" should be "restore[d] ... gently" (NIV). They should be cared for with intentionality; their burdens should be shared. We might limit burden-bearing to sorrows and griefs, and it certainly applies to them, but it is also relevant to your sin struggle. It applies to your sin of addictive habits, too.

Change becomes increasingly possible as friends, family members, counselors, and pastors help us to grow, fight, and carry on. Victor had been through our addiction counseling program twice, yet he remained stuck in a cycle of sin. As he entered his third round of counseling, we invited a member of his small group, Fred, to start helping out. Fred wasn't a trained counselor.

He was a godly friend whose influence made a huge difference. He called Victor regularly, spent weekends with him, worked on projects together with him, and challenged him to grow in godliness. They talked about Victor's addictive habit, but they also talked about marriage, parenting, work, Scripture, and countless other things. When Victor was discouraged, he called Fred. When he was tempted, he drove to Fred's house. When he was angry, he asked Fred for prayer. Over time, their relationship became a vital part of helping Victor to overcome his struggle.

Are you struggling to let go of an addictive habit? Have you made your struggle worse by isolating yourself? Are you fighting alone? Not only is it the responsibility of others to help bear your burden, it is your responsibility to ask others to share in it. You need them. The apostle James gives us an incentive to share when he tells us that confessing our sins to one another can be a step toward healing (see James 5:16). Healing requires helping hands—so who is helping to bear your burden?

Reflect: "Whoever isolates himself seeks his own desire; he breaks out against all sound judgment" (Prov. 18:1).

Reflect: Isolation makes addiction worse. Who can you turn to for help? Who can you call today?

Act: Make a list of the people who are helping you to fight sin and temptation. How are they helping you? Thank God for partners in the fight against your addiction. Where do you still need help? Ask your friends for assistance in areas where you are still struggling.

RESTRUCTURING

Addictive habits become so embedded in our lives that even when we are ready to stop them it can feel daunting. Change must take into consideration strategic moves that will restructure our lives to help us build up momentum and avoid temptation. This section will invite you to meditate on ways that you can develop a strategic relapse prevention plan.

DAY 18

Cut It Out

If your right eye causes you to sin, tear it out and throw it away. For it is better that you lose one of your members than that your whole body be thrown into hell. And if your right hand causes you to sin, cut it off and throw it away. For it is better that you lose one of your members than that your whole body go into hell. (Matt. 5:29–30)

IT FELT LIKE cutting off an arm, but for Everett to truly make progress in his battle against porn, he had to give up his smartphone. As a technology geek, he not only loved his phone but had become dependent on it for many things. That phone, however, was also his sole source of porn on a daily basis. It had to go. The fight against temptation calls for dramatic action.

Jesus's language is bold. He tells his hearers to remove their hands and eyes if they cause them to sin. Yet self-mutilation is not what Jesus intends. After all, one-eyed and one-handed individuals can still lust. Jesus speaks hyperbolically, exaggerating for effect. He shows how decisive and dramatic our action should be when we are tempted. You can't passively fight your sin. You have to take *radical steps* to cut your addiction out of your life.

Jesus's choice of hand and eye are not unintentional. These parts are often linked to lust and adultery—the issue that Jesus is most keen to address. But most of us use our hands and eyes every day—even every moment of our waking hours. To lose these parts is not simply inconvenient; it means *a complete overhaul of the way we do life*. Remember that Jesus calls us to dramatic action. No matter how convenient or necessary something is, if causes you to sin against God, cut it out!

Victory doesn't come easily. You must include a plan to restructure your life in order to avoid temptations. We can't, of course, avoid every temptation, but there are many you can cut out in order to strengthen your resolve and build momentum toward victory. Creating new routines, developing new habits, and making different choices can go a long way. These things help us to avoid tempting spots, people, and things.

This looks different for everyone. For Carlos it meant getting rid of his computer, and for Jeff it meant cancelling his cable subscription. For Sharon it meant cutting up her credit card. For Devan it included turning in his receipts to an accountability partner. For Wilma it meant driving the long way to work and avoiding certain roads. For Bobby it meant changing his phone number so that old friends couldn't contact him anymore, and for Elijah it meant disconnecting from social media. There are countless ways to restructure your life in order to avoid temptation, but this will require dramatic and intentional action. Are you prepared to take a drastic step to cut sin out of your life?

Reflect: With God's help, you can take a radical step. What would that be for you?

Reflect: What temptation do you need to cut out of your life?

Act: Write out a strategy for avoiding the most common temptations that you experience. Share your plan with a trusted friend or counselor.

DAY 19

Trigger Warning

So that we would not be outwitted by Satan; for we
are not ignorant of his designs. (2 Cor. 2:11)

PAULO'S DISCONTENT WAS a problem. Prolonged grumbling increased his temptation to look at porn. The more aware of this trigger he became, the more equipped he was to head off the temptations. Knowing our triggers is a vital step in fighting our addictive habits.

Satan has schemes and designs. He has a battle plan. Paul observes that knowing Satan's designs allows us not to be "outwitted" by him. The apostle warns the Corinthians that unwillingness to forgive a repentant brother provides Satan a foothold in the church (see 2 Cor. 2:5–10). By being aware of this, the Corinthians could take direct action against Satan's scheme. We fight better when we know the enemy's plan of attack. This requires two things: that we know both the enemy's standard MO and our own weakness.

Day 15 addressed the two common schemes of the devil: temptation and accusation. But that's not all Satan does. Satan loves to undermine your hope, discourage your efforts at recovery, and cause you to doubt God's goodness. He also tries to hide God's justice and God's love from us. If you know this, you can counteract the devil by focusing more earnestly on these aspects of God. Highlighting his justice reminds you to do what is right. Highlighting his love invites you to repent when you don't do what is right.

You must also know your weaknesses. Satan knows our weaknesses and seeks to exploit them. If, as in Paulo's case, grumbling becomes a point of temptation, then Satan encourages discontentment. But as Paulo worked to cultivate gratitude, he was more prepared to fight off the enemy's attack.

What are some triggers that tempt you to give in to your addictive habit? Are there any patterns to your sin (a time of day, place, mood, and so on)? What precedes your failures? What are you thinking, wanting, or doing before you give in? Answering these questions can help you identify potential triggers. Some common experiences that trigger an addiction are loneliness, stress, bitterness, entitlement, and fatigue. Do any of these themes appear in your struggle?

Consider your heart and your weaknesses. When you know how Satan might attack you, you can better plan a defense. Be prepared to counteract his schemes. So, for example, if *fatigue* is a common trigger for you, make a plan to get better rest. If *entitlement* is a common trigger, engage in more service projects at church. If *bitterness* is poisoning your heart, work at forgiving. If *loneliness* has taken over your life, turn first to God and then initiate with friends at church. Don't be outwitted by your enemy. Know his schemes and develop a defensive plan to fight against temptation.

Reflect: Keep in mind the apostle Peter's warning: "Be sober-minded; be watchful. Your adversary the devil prowls around like a roaring lion, seeking someone to devour" (1 Peter 5:8).

Reflect: How might Satan be using your own weaknesses against you? What can you do to develop a defensive plan against temptation?

Act: Journal your temptations. Visit afresh the context of your temptation and identify any triggers.

DAY 20

Confess!

Therefore, confess your sins to one another and pray for one another, that you may be healed. The prayer of a righteous person has great power as it is working. (James 5:16)

REPENTANCE IS NOT a *one-time* event, as if we confess our sins and turn from them and then all is changed. Rather, confession and repentance are *regular* and *repeated* events as believers grow in holiness. Confessing our sins regularly to one another is an important aspect of change.

A colleague of mine has often said, "You are only as free as you are honest." This beautiful statement captures well the bondage of hiding our sins. Fear of exposure builds walls between us and others, and between us and God. The more we fear being found out, the more distance we create and the more we avoid certain people and topics. As we hide our sin, we become increasingly enslaved to it. Sin grows in the darkness, just like mold. Your addictive habits must be brought into the light. Stop hiding your addiction. Confess to others your fears, failures, and struggles.

James tells us that *through confession real healing can begin.* Confession results in both exposure and intercession. Sin loves the darkness. In the dark, it lies to you. It says, "It's not that big a deal" or "You are still in control" or "You aren't hurting anyone" or "No one can relate to your problems." But when you expose your sin you rob it of all its deceptive power. When you bring sin into the light you reveal it, own it, and tell others that you're ready to change.

Confession leads to help. When we confess our sins, others can intercede on our behalf and can pray that God might give us the strength to fight sin. James says that we confess our sins in order that we may be healed. The prayers of other believers have tremendous power. God delights to answer the prayers of his children when they pray for one another. Confession invites others to fight with you, to pray for your fight against sin. This begins a pathway toward healing.

I saw this most memorably in the life of Sarah, who was a part of my small group for many years. Her secret spending habits had resulted in thousands of dollars of debt. Sarah managed to keep this a secret from her husband for nearly three years, but guilt was eating her up inside. When we talked about confession of sin, the Lord pricked her conscience and urged her to confess. When she did, a flood of grace and help resulted. Not only did confession ease her conscience, but it allowed healing to begin on multiple levels. She was honest with her husband. Small group members prayed for her. And a team of people helped her to develop a financial plan to address her debt.

Are there habits, temptations, or failures that you've been hiding? Confess your sins, friend, that you may be healed.

Reflect: Are you scared to confess? What stops you from being honest?

Reflect: Who can you regularly share your struggles and failures with? Who can you invite to pray for your fight against addictive habits?

Act: Write a confession letter about anything you have not confessed. Share what you've done with a few important people in your life. Ask for forgiveness, if you've sinned against them, and for their prayer support.

DAY 21

Flee Temptation

So flee youthful passions and pursue righteousness, faith, love, and peace, along with those who call on the Lord from a pure heart. (2 Tim. 2:22)

THERE ARE FAR too many temptations that we can't *avoid*, but there are temptations that we can *evade*. A recovering alcoholic can't avoid every beer ad on television, but he can stay out of the bar. For the apostle Paul, fleeing temptation has two key components: running *from* and running *toward*.

Paul speaks of fleeing "youthful passions." In context, the phrase points to the rebelliousness and contentiousness that drive a young man to stir up conflict (see 2 Tim. 2:23–26). We can apply the principle of fleeing youthful passions to all sins, including addictive habits. Addictions are often characterized by youthful impulsivity and arrogance and are also grounded in selfishness and immediacy.

Paul's command to flee should be heeded, regardless of the nature of our sin. Are you ready to run? What's holding you back? We must run as fast and as far as we can from these passions, desires, and impulses.

Start with fleeing *temptation*. I can't help but think of young Joseph, who ran so fast that he left his clothes in the unrelenting grip of Potiphar's wife (see Gen. 39)! That's desperation and determination. So also for you—you must run from temptations, run from the passions and desires that would lead you to self-indulgence.

Paul doesn't simply say to flee youthful passion, but he adds, "Pursue righteousness, faith, love, and peace." We are always running toward something. What we are running toward should be godly and good for us. We can fight temptation best when we are replacing it with the character of righteousness, the confidence of faith in Christ, the love of God and others, and the peace that seeks unity with one another. As we put *off* youthful passions, we put *on* righteousness, faith, love, and peace (see Eph. 4:22–24). This is what transformation looks like in the Christian life.

Good news: you don't do this alone. You have fellow believers jogging alongside you like running partners in a marathon. "So flee . . . and pursue . . . *along with* those who call on the Lord from a pure heart." Find those who are living self-controlled, pure, and godly lives (see Titus 1:7–9; 2:1–8). Ask them to help you.

We must run from temptation, but we must also run toward godliness. What are you running toward? If it isn't Christ, you will likely only replace one sinful habit with a different one. Flee temptation by pursuing godliness in your life.

Reflect: What temptations, bad habits, and sins *must* you flee right now? What stops you from running from them? What might it look like for you to run away? Be specific.

Reflect: What might it look like for you to pursue godliness? In what ways do you need to grow? How can faith, love, and peace become more a part of your life? Again, be specific in your answers.

Act: Godliness concerns more than just your addictive habit. Consider one area of your spiritual life, apart from your addictive habit, that needs attention. Make a plan for how you are going to pursue godliness in that area. Find a pastor, counselor, or trusted friend and share your plan with him or her.

DAY 22

When You Can't Avoid It

I have learned in whatever situation I am to be content. I know how to be brought low, and I know how to abound. In any and every circumstance, I have learned the secret of facing plenty and hunger, abundance and need. I can do all things through him who strengthens me. (Phil. 4:11–13)

IT WOULD BE great if we could *always* avoid temptation. We would *never* fear sliding back into sinful habits or failing to change. That isn't how the world works, however. God *never* promises a temptation-free life. In fact, Jesus warns that we will have many troubles (see John 16:33). Do you know how to adapt to the many difficulties and temptations that life poses?

What is a godly response to hardships, stress, pressure, and temptation? Paul models this well. In his letter to the Philippians, he notes some situations that he has faced—each different, sometimes dramatically different, from the other. Yet he responds in a way that honors God, regardless of the situation. Whether he is "low" or "abounding," he can be content. He has "learned in whatever situation" how to have a right, God-honoring response. Here's the key: Paul *learned* to be content, regardless of the circumstances. This attitude didn't come naturally. He worked at it. What good news! If Paul can learn contentment, *so can you.*

Situations that may trigger an addictive habit are too numerous to avoid. But you can learn a godly response to unexpected difficulties and temptations. Here are three suggestions.

Have a simple plan. Your plan should include fighting for contentment, running from temptation, and running to godly friends. Do you know who you can call when things get difficult? Have you communicated to this person that you need his or her help and need to call when you're in trouble? Has he or she agreed to be there for you? Don't simply react to your problems. Be proactive and prepared. Plan what to do *before* difficult moments strike.

Expect hardships, stress, and temptation to keep coming. After a season of victory, it's common to let your guard down. "I got this," you think. In that moment of vulnerability, sin strikes. Expect temptation to continue. Don't celebrate before the war is over. If you're realistic about sin, you will keep your defenses up and stay on guard. Learn to honor God with vigilance and sober judgment about life in a fallen world (see Rom. 12:2–3).

Reevaluate regularly. If you identify cracks in your plan, stop and address them. Regularly take stock of how you're doing. Has temptation changed? Is it more frequent? Is it more common when you are in *certain* places, with *certain* people, thinking about *certain* things? Did you remember something about your addictive lifestyle that you had forgotten? Be willing to stop and confront any issues. Reevaluating your plan and making changes is crucial to sustained progress.

Paul models a godly attitude and response to difficulties. And so can you, because you can do "all things through Christ who strengthens [you]." Christ can help you. Make your plans, expect hardships and temptations, and reevaluate regularly—but look to Jesus most of all.

Reflect: You can learn to be content, just like Paul did. Do you actually believe this?

Reflect: Think strategically. When is temptation most likely to come?

Act: Make an emergency speed-dial list of people you can call when difficulties and temptations strike.

DAY 23

Growing in Humility

But he gives more grace. Therefore it says, "God opposes the proud but gives grace to the humble." (James 4:6)

THE PROUD PERSON never really changes. He may not change because he is too arrogant to believe that he needs to change. Or she may recognize the need, but her pride keeps her from listening to the wisdom and counsel of those who can offer her help. Change in your life will require you to grow in humility.

James draws a straight line from humility to God's grace. God "gives grace to the humble." To the degree that you are humble, God will give more and more grace to help you. Humility draws grace because humility admits that we are not God and that we need him. A humble person sees himself as the Bible advises. He does not think more highly of himself than he ought (see Rom. 12:3). So, as we cultivate humility, we find that God's grace abounds to us. He is ready to help those who are willing to admit that they need him.

What does cultivating humility look like? We don't often think about how to become more humble, but there are things we can do to grow in this quality. James tells us to draw near to God (see James 4:8), which means acknowledging that you are not God. It means submitting to him (see v. 7) and surrendering your own selfish demands (see vv. 1–3). Humility is directly tied to our nearness to God. The closer you grow to the Lord, the more humble you will become.

Apply this to your struggle. The proud person insists that he doesn't need any help or doesn't need to change. The proud person insists that she should be able to do recovery her way, on her terms, in her time. The proud person demands that he get what he wants, when he wants it. The humble person, however, knows that without God she can never truly change. She knows that change will come when, and at whatever pace, God grants it. The humble person doesn't make demands of God but surrenders to his will and his way.

What would humility look like in your life? Where can you see evidence of pride? How can you draw closer to God in an effort to cultivate humility? Remember that if you are proud, God opposes you. You will never change. If, however, you are humble and you draw near to God, he too will draw near to you (see v. 8). God loves to give grace to those who ask rightly of him (see vv. 2–3). Will you humble yourself? Will you cry out to God for the grace that you need to fight your addictive habit?

Reflect: What do you think of when you think of humility? Read Philippians 2:5–11. How does the humility of Christ lead to salvation? How can this verse motivate you to pursue humility in your life?

Act: List the areas of your life in which you are most prone to pride. How can you turn those areas of your life into a means to draw closer to God?

DAY 24

Finding New Joy

They shall not build and another inhabit; they shall not plant and another eat; for like the days of a tree shall the days of my people be, and my chosen shall long enjoy the work of their hands. (Isa. 65:22)

GOD IS NOT A KILLJOY! When an addiction takes deep root in our life, it often becomes the only way that we experience any fun and pleasure. To lose it, then, is not simply to lose a habit but to lose our only "good thing." So we conclude that God is a spoilsport. He does not care about our joy—just our obedience. But God *does* want joy for us—he wants it, however, in the right places.

Today's reading focuses on God's desire for his people to enjoy their lives. He speaks of enjoying "the work of their hands." God wants them to enjoy their homes, their cities, their crops. In fact, he wants them to *long* enjoy these fruits. "Again you shall plant vineyards on the mountains of Samaria; the planters shall plant and shall enjoy the fruit" (Jer. 31:5). God is for our joy.

Yet this joy must be found within its proper place. Our addictive habits seek pleasure through sinful indulgence. God sets boundaries on our joy. He is not out to squelch our fun. He knows that real joy is found within the safety of submitting to his will. Remember, also, that God speaks of joy that results from the "work" of his people's hands. Joy often comes in conjunction with your hard work. If you are fighting an addictive habit, joy can come as you labor to put your sin to death. A more secure joy can return to your life.

If an addictive habit has been your primary means of plea-sure, then with hard work you should anticipate the cultivation of new joys. It's not easy to say no to what has previously given you pleasure; in fact, other so-called joys may seem banal and empty. Learning to find the joy in the "banal" will be hard work, but it will eventually result in real enjoyment.

I love the way that one recovering alcoholic says it. In an article from Quartz, Kristi Coulter describes her second summer of sobriety. As she sits by the pool, a group of obviously drunk girls jump in for a swim, drinking all the while. She sits on the opposite side of the pool and describes her sense of simple pleasure: "It is *so* nice on this side of the pool, where the book I'm reading is a letdown and my legs look too white and the ice has long since melted in my glass and work is hard and there's still no good way to be a girl and I don't know what to do with my life and I have to actually deal with all of that. I never expected to make it to this side of the pool. I can't believe I get to be here."[1]

Change must involve more than simply saying no to bad things. It must also involve saying yes to good things. It involves finding satisfaction in the mundane and normal things of life. And in these things you find a different—dare I say better—kind of joy. What are the healthy joys that you can engage in?

Reflect: The great king David says, "You [God] make known to me the path of life; in your presence there is fullness of joy; at your right hand are pleasures forevermore" (Ps. 16:11). Do you hear that? The Lord offers more than temporary joy. He holds out a fullness of joy that is even better than the momentary pleasures of your addiction. His pleasures are "forevermore." The greatest joy of all is found in God's presence.

Act: Try one new thing—something that sounds fun but is unfamiliar to you. Invite a friend to tag along.

DAY 25

The Power of Awe

And we all, with unveiled face, beholding the glory of the Lord, are
being transformed into the same image from one degree of glory to
another. For this comes from the Lord who is the Spirit. (2 Cor. 3:18)

HAVE YOU EVER been in awe of something? Perhaps a beautiful sunset? Or maybe a trip to the Grand Canyon impressed on
you the need to stop and just gaze in wonderment? There is power
in awe, and there is nothing more awe-inspiring than the God of
glory and grace. Turning from our addictive habits requires us to
be increasingly in awe of God.

In this verse, Paul writes about two interrelated ideas: awe and
transformation. He speaks first of encountering the glory of the
Lord with "unveiled face." This harks back to Moses, who encoun-
tered God's glory when he removed the veil from his face (see
2 Cor. 3:13). Paul speaks of you—a Christian—encountering this
glory directly. Because of Jesus, we can enter into the presence of
God (see Rom. 5:2) and behold his glory.

Paul also speaks about our transformation from "one degree
of glory to another." This is an unfolding progression. The more
we behold the amazing beauty of the Lord, the more in awe we
become, and then the more we are "transformed into the same
image." We never encounter the glory of the Lord and remain the
same. As we are awed by God, our desires change, our thoughts
alter, and our activities adjust. When I am astonished by something, it compels a response from me. So the beautiful sunset, the
one that really stuns me, causes me to pull over and stop and gaze.
Taking a moment is more important than arriving at my next des-
tination. I take action: I pull the car over, take out my camera, and
capture the moment. Admiring this beauty matters more to me

than the convenience of uninterrupted travel. Awe is powerful. Awe changes how I live.

For far too long, your addictive habit has captured your attention and affections. What can be done about it? How about studying the beauty of the Lord? Admiring his excellence and attributes? Fight back against temptations and sin by immersing yourself in the character of God, the beauty of the gospel, and the glory of Jesus Christ. Study, pray, sing, and talk over these things with friends. At every turn, make it your mission to grow in your awe of God and of Jesus, his beloved son. The more you "behold," the more you will be transformed.

Reflect: What things about God and the gospel amaze you? Why?

Reflect: Be in awe of Jesus—he offers you forgiveness (see Eph. 1:7), cleansing (see Heb. 10:22), justification (see Rom. 4:25), and access to God (see Eph. 3:12).

Act: Study your Bible—especially the gospels. Pray the Psalms. Listen to compelling worship music. Talk with friends about your salvation story. There are hundreds of ways to become enamored with the glory of God. Make a list of the things you can do to grow in your experience of "beholding the glory of the Lord." Then pick a few and begin your pursuit of God.

REMAINING

Your battle with an addictive habit doesn't stop once you are past the climax of the struggle. Change requires careful and strategic consideration about how to remain faithful in the long run. This section will invite you to meditate on how you can plan for faithfulness in your life over time.

DAY 26

Don't Return

Like a dog that returns to his vomit is a fool
who repeats his folly. (Prov. 26:11)

WHAT A GROSS IMAGE! I have seen dogs do this, and it's as disgusting as it sounds. Dogs, of course, don't know any better. The fool ought to know better, but he returns to his foolishness anyway. It is ridiculous to return to your sin when you have made progress against it. As you make progress in your fight, you must learn how to *not* be the fool.

The fool never learns from his mistakes. He encounters consequences for his sins but still persists in them. The quintessential example of this is Pharaoh. He stubbornly refused to let Israel go, and he faced consequences in the form of horrific plagues. He relented and agreed to let them go, but once the punishment abated he returned to his rebellion (see Ex. 8:15). Or consider the alcoholic in Proverbs 23. This drunkard hallucinates (see v. 33), gets into fights and falls down, and does not feel pain when hit (see v. 35). His response when he awakes from his drunken stupor is to "have another drink." Despite all the negative consequences, fools, like the vomit-eating dog, return to their folly.

The truth is that negative consequences alone are not enough to cause us to stop sinning. If that were the case, then no one would become addicted. In fact, a habit that continues despite adverse consequences is one of the key features that defines an addiction. Learning not to be the fool, then, involves more than awareness of personal consequences. It involves turning to the Lord and giving your life to him.

The Bible has a lot to say about fools. It speaks of the fool's relationship to God and to others. The psalmist indicted the fool for his lack of faith in God. A fool literally says in his heart, "There is no God" (Ps. 14:1; 53:1) and casts aspersions on the Lord's worth and character (see Ps. 74:18, 22). To be the fool, to return to your folly, is to regard your relationship with God as an inferior and insignificant thing. *Remaining diligent in the fight, then, requires you to stay close to the Lord.* Keep your heart and mind fixed on him through prayer, study, and worship.

The fool also disregards others. The fool "despises wisdom" (see Prov. 1:7, 22) and refuses to listen to counsel (see Prov. 12:15; 15:5; 23:9). Do you disregard wise counsel from godly people? Stay close to wise counselors. Be humble enough to hear them, and apply biblical wisdom to your problems. And note this: accountability and counseling don't end when the climax of your struggle has passed. You will need partners to help you fight for faith. None of us can survive on our own.

Along with progress will come temptations to relax our efforts against sin. Pride strikes at such moments (see Prov. 16:18). We think to ourselves, *Just one more time* or *I can handle it now* or *I've earned a little fun.* But to return to our addictive habit at that moment is foolishness. Stay close to God and close to godly people and you won't be the fool.

Reflect: What does foolishness look like in your life? How can you stay close to God and godly people?

Reflect: Don't give up. Jesus came to rescue fools.

Act: Write a letter to yourself listing the reasons that it would be foolish to return to your addictive habit. Then share it with a trusted friend.

DAY 27

Steward Your Whole Life

And whatever you do, in word or deed, do everything in the name of the Lord Jesus, giving thanks to God the Father through him. (Col. 3:17)

ADDICTIVE HABITS CREATE all kinds of problems, impacting our honesty, relationships, finances, health, and more. Sarah hid her new purchases in the garage and waited until everyone was at work or school before bringing them into the house. Lying to her family was as big a part of her sin as spending was. Stephen spent so many nights drinking in his basement that he missed nearly every significant event in his children's lives for two years. His kids resented him. Sobriety was not his only problem.

Our sin often deceives us into thinking that our only problem is our addiction. "If I can just get my drinking under control . . ." "If I can just stop buying so much junk . . ." "If I can just overcome my lust . . ." These phrases suggest that our only struggle is our addictive habit. If we can just deal with it, we'll be good. In truth, your addiction isn't your only problem. Sarah was overspending, but she was also lying to her family. Stephen was a drunkard, but his kids also hated him. Spiritual growth comes when we take responsibility for *our whole lives*, not just our addictions.

Paul starts today's verse by saying, "Whatever you do." He gives as broad a picture of our lives as he can. Then he adds "in word or deed." Not a single area of our lives is untouched by the lordship of Christ.

Paul adds, "Do everything in the name of the Lord Jesus." As we take responsibility for our whole lives, we are called to do everything to the glory of God (see 1 Cor. 10:31). No aspect of our lives can escape the lordship of Christ. Our goal is to honor Jesus everywhere and in every setting (see 2 Cor. 5:9). This might seem unrealistic, but it is possible through the grace and strength that Christ gives.

How has your addictive habit impacted your life? Remaining vigilant requires you to address a variety of areas in your life. Who has been impacted by your addiction? What do you need to take responsibility for and begin to address differently? How can you steward your whole life? Stewardship refers to our oversight or management of things. We speak often in the church of "stewarding our finances," which means managing our money in a way that is consistent with God's desires. How can you manage all your life in a way that is consistent with God's desires for you?

Paul finishes today's verse with "giving thanks to God the Father through him." Thankfulness is an attitude that recognizes God's goodness. Anything good in our lives comes from God (see James 1:17). Every word and deed, everything we do, must be accompanied with thankfulness to God. You might look at your life and think, *I've got nothing to thank him for* . . . But, through Christ, thankfulness is possible. Christ died for you, so that sin would no longer blind you to God's goodness. A *humble* and *grateful* heart acknowledges his goodness, no matter how bad circumstances are.

Reflect: What areas of your life have been impacted by your addictive habit? How can you put every aspect of your life under the lordship of Christ?

Reflect: How can you express thanks to God through Christ?

Act: Pick an area of your life that has been impacted by your addictive habit, and develop a plan, with help from others, for how to address it. Do you need marriage counseling? Should you write a repentance letter? Do you need a medical consult? What else might you need to do?

DAY 28

The Power of Gratitude

*But sexual immorality and all impurity or covetousness must not
even be named among you, as is proper among saints. Let there
be no filthiness nor foolish talk nor crude joking, which are out
of place, but instead let there be thanksgiving. (Eph. 5:3–4)*

ON DAY 27, we explored thankfulness as an attitude that recognizes God's goodness. Today we go one step further: thankfulness is a weapon to fight your addiction.

We don't usually think of thankfulness as a spiritual weapon.
But since nearly all sin is rooted in selfishness, gratitude becomes
a means of fighting against temptation. When our addictive habits
tell us that *we need more*, thankfulness reminds us that *we already
have more than we deserve*. There is power in gratitude.

In Ephesians 5:3–4, Paul encourages putting off sinful habits and replacing them with thankfulness. The addicted heart is
greedy for more: more alcohol, more shoes, more money, more
attention, more sex, more food. The very nature of greed is that
it can't see beyond what it covets. It's so preoccupied with what
it wants that it's blind to what God has already given.[1] Thankfulness is the opposite of greed. It is so overcome with gratitude for
God's goodness that it can't help but thank him. Thankfulness,
then, becomes a weapon for our warfare.

Consider worry. What does worry say? It says, "I need . . ."
Worry thinks it needs more than what God is giving at the present moment. Worry is dissatisfied with what God is doing, what
God has said, and what God has promised. It needs more—more
certainty, more immediacy, more satisfaction. But thankfulness
robs worry of its greediness. It turns it on its head, pointing us to

all that God has given us and reassuring us of his continued care and provision (see Rom. 8:32).

Consider anger. Anger says, "I didn't get what I wanted; therefore, I am going to respond with bitterness and rage." Sinful anger wells from a heart that has warring passions (see James 4:1–2). Anger springs from a discontent heart. But thankfulness reminds us that all that we have we have received from God—and that none of it we deserve. An attitude of thankfulness remembers the myriads of blessings that come from the Lord's hands. Thankfulness robs anger of its power. A thankful heart has no room to breed bitterness and rage.

Whatever your addictive habit, it insists that you need more and that you need things that God won't provide for you. Thankfulness, however, recognizes that I deserve hell and yet God gives me grace. God abounds in grace (see 2 Cor. 9:8) and invites us to rejoice in all that he gives. Paul even asks the Corinthians, "What do you have that you did not receive?" (1 Cor. 4:7). The answer is "nothing." Every good thing that we have comes from God (see James 1:17); and, whatever struggles we face, we still have much good in our lives. So fight against the greed of temptation by celebrating God kindness, grace, love, and generosity to you.

The greatest act of God's love was sending his Son to die for our sins (see Rom. 5:8) and to rescue us from hell (see Rom. 8:1). For that, we should all be eternally thankful (see 2 Thess. 2:13).

Reflect: In what ways are you greedy for more? What do you want? What do you covet? What has God already given you that you don't care about or give credence to?

Act: Set a timer for three minutes, and in that time write as many things as you can think of for which to be thankful. Do this several times a week in order to cultivate an attitude of gratitude.

DAY 29

You Belong to God

Once you were not a people, but now you are God's people; once you had not received mercy, but now you have received mercy. (1 Peter 2:10)

LONELINESS CAN BE debilitating. The reason many people get sucked into addictive habits is to dull the silence. Alcohol becomes a social lubricant and makes you the life of the party. Drugs become a communal activity. Shopping consoles your feelings of rejection. Your addictive habits have countless connections with your longing for acceptance.

When we realize, however, that God accepts us in Christ, everything changes. God's acceptance provides hope and motivates endurance in the face of temptation.

The Christians in Asia Minor knew something about trials, hardships, and sufferings (see 1 Peter 1:6). They knew something about temptation, too. When Peter writes to them, they are experiencing all kinds of persecution—many of them being exiled from their homes and families (see v. 1). In this context, far from home and feeling the pressures of exile, they would find it tempting to indulge in sin. Peter encourages them to "abstain from the passions of the flesh" (1 Peter 2:11) and to live honorably before others. Their honorable lifestyle is to be motivated by their honored identity. "Once you were not a people, but now you are God's people."

Addictive habits can create relational problems. They have probably also provoked insecurity in you and, with that, feelings of shame and embarrassment. It is tempting to dwell on broken relationships, insecurity, and personal shame. While you ought to give these issues consideration, if you remain stuck on them, you will return to your addictions in order to mitigate their pain. You

79

ought to instead focus on the acceptance that is offered to you in Christ. Do you believe that God accepts you? Do you believe you are one of "God's people"? *Identity drives obedience.* When you realize who you are in Christ, you are compelled to live out that identity. God accepts you through Christ and makes you one of his people. Now your responsibility is to own that acceptance and relish in your new identity.

Peter speaks too of your receiving Christ's mercy. We aren't made God's people because we are worthy of such a privilege. You may look at the history of your addictive habit—the broken relationships, the hurtful words, the lies and deceptions, the reckless living—and you may say, "I can't be one of God's people." If your acceptance were based on what you have done, you would be right. None of us gets to be among God's people by virtue of what we do (see Rom. 2:23). We are each made a child of God by mercy. "Once you had not received mercy, but now," in Christ, "you have received mercy" (1 Peter 2:10). That is God's message for you! Now that you are his child, mercy overflows into your life.

You once lived apart from God and without his mercy. But now God's acceptance and mercy transform and sustain your life. They drive you to fight. They provide hope when you are tempted to give up. They remind you that you belong to God. They help you to no longer fill your solitude and loneliness with cheap versions of acceptance.

Reflect: Do you believe that God accepts you? If not, what gets in your way? What stops you from believing this truth?

Reflect: How can your identity in Christ motivate your obedience?

Act: Read Ephesians 1 and 2 and list everything that the text says about the Christian. Use these verses to remind yourself of who you are in Christ.

DAY 30

Don't Run from Hardship

Not only that, but we rejoice in our sufferings, knowing that
suffering produces endurance, and endurance produces character,
and character produces hope, and hope does not put us to shame,
because God's love has been poured into our hearts through
the Holy Spirit who has been given to us. (Rom. 5:3–5)

I MUST HAVE heard it a thousand times growing up: hard work builds character. It was often said after a significant snowfall when I was being told to shovel the driveway. We hear it in all sorts of other settings, too—on the ball field, in the classroom, at the gym, and on the job. We also hear it in Scripture: Don't fear hardship. Run from sin, but don't run from trials.

In Romans 5, the apostle Paul tells us that believers have peace with God (see v. 1) and access to God through faith and that they "rejoice in hope of the glory of God" (v. 2). Peace, access, and hope in glory—all wonderful blessings of justification. Paul then makes an abrupt transition in verse 3. Shockingly, he tells us to rejoice in our sufferings as well. Paul is not a masochist—it's not that the apostle enjoys pain. Rather, he knows that *the pain of suffering can have transformative results when hardship is stewarded well.* Suffering can change you for good. When we steward hardship well, we can see the benefits of endurance, character, and hope.

Endurance is the strengthening of our faith. When our faith endures despite hardship, we know what we truly believe. If your faith is never tested, you don't know whether you really love God or just love what God does for you. But suffering gives you a chance to test your faith.

As you endure, you also grow your *character*. As our faith grows, we begin to look more like Jesus. Our character can change through suffering. We learn patience through suffering. We learn the difference between joy and happiness. We learn to sacrifice. We learn countless lessons and develop our character in tons of little ways through hardship.

Finally, as your character changes, so does your *hope*. Hope increases through suffering. Suffering always attacks what you love. Previously, when suffering happened, your response was to run to an addictive habit in order to comfort yourself. But when your hope is transferred to an "eternal weight of glory" (2 Cor. 4:17), suffering can't touch hope. Instead suffering cultivates an ever-increasing longing for that glory.

Overcoming an addictive habit is not an escape from all hardship and trial. "In this world you will have trouble," says Jesus (John 16:33 NIV). If you attempt to run from it all, you will either fall back into an addictive habit or simply create some other unhealthy means of escapism. Don't run from hardship, but instead view it as an opportunity. View hardships as the spiritual gym that can lead to strength in your Christian life. It can lead to a stronger faith, a more Christ-like character, and a deeper hope. Change your perspective on hardship, and you can grow through it.

Reflect: What difficulty are you trying to run from? Why? How can you view it as a spiritual strengthening opportunity?

Act: Overcoming an addictive habit is a trial. Make a list of the ways in which God has already used this experience to grow your spiritual life.

DAY 31

The Grace That Endures

For the LORD is good; his steadfast love endures forever,
and his faithfulness to all generations. (Ps. 100:5)

YOU HAVE COME to the end of this book, but you have not come to the end of your journey. Much still lies ahead of you: a growing hope as you struggle against addictive habits, more faith in Christ, greater endurance as you suffer. But for all that is good that lies ahead, there is also much temptation, sadness, anger, frustration, disappointment, and even failure. This is not the end of the story. Here's the good news: you have not come to the end of God's grace. God's grace endures forever.

The author of Psalm 100 encourages the reader to rejoice in God—to give thanks and praise to him. He tells us why. We ought to praise him because he is God (see v. 3a), because he made us (see v. 3b), because he watches over us like a good shepherd (see v. 3c), and because he is good (see v. 5). Verse 5, then, unpacks what it means to speak of God's goodness.

The psalmist begins by describing God's *enduring love*. There is a hint of redundancy in the structure: he has steadfast love that endures forever. Grammatically speaking, it's not necessary to say that this love both is "steadfast" and "endures forever." To be steadfast is to endure. Yet the psalmist knows precisely what he is writing. He wants to stress just how enduring this love is. God's love is committed to us, and that love never runs out. God's commitment to love his people is a forever commitment. It's a love you can rest in.

The psalmist then adds that God also has an *enduring faithfulness*. His commitment isn't limited to one generation; it goes down through history to all those who are his. The enduring love of God is not reserved for the saints of the Old Testament. It is not limited to the author of this Psalm. It is not even restricted to the apostles in the New Testament. God's enduring love is for you too. Centuries after this psalm was written, we can still claim these words as our hope and promise.

God's grace started you on this journey, and it is God's grace that will carry you onward in it. You never escape your need of his grace, and because of his goodness you never have to fear that you will lose it. Trust that, whatever the next step is for you, God's grace will meet you there and empower you to take it. His "steadfast love endures forever." In the words of John Newton, "'Tis grace has brought me safe thus far, and grace will lead me home."[1]

Reflect: What do you most fear about the future of your walk with the Lord? How can you trust God's grace to help you face it?

Act: God provides grace to us in thousands of ways, but primarily he offers it through our studying Scripture, praying, and fellowshipping with the church. Make a plan for how you are going to grow in these spiritual disciplines. What will you study in Scripture? When will you pray? What will your participation in church look like? If you are not sure how to answer these questions, find a godly friend who can help you.

Conclusion

No one plans to become addicted. You didn't wake up one morning and decide that you would like food or drugs to control your life. You didn't determine to become an alcoholic or set out to be ruled by video games. Whatever journey brought you to this point, it often feels like it will never get better. The slavery of an addictive habit can be intense and discouraging. But there is still hope that you can change.

It is unlikely that this 31-day devotional has brought you to a point of freedom. It is certainly possible, but it is unlikely. Change is more difficult than reading a devotional and doing some exercises. Addictive habits in particular spread to every corner of our lives, picking up more and more cues along the way, which makes them particularly difficult to root out.[1] You should expect the fight against an addictive habit to be difficult.

On the one hand, perhaps you read through this book and did every day and every assignment as instructed. Maybe you feel like you're really changing. Rejoice in that, and celebrate what God might be doing, but don't let your guard down. Stay humble about your potential to fall back into sin. Damian was convinced after a few weeks that he had finally "turned the corner." "This time," he kept saying, "everything is different." There were lots of reasons to rejoice, and I was thrilled for him when he attained a month of sobriety—but with success came a relaxed vigilance. Eventually he started missing appointments, stopped attending our weekly substance-abuse meeting, and before long fell back into sin. Small victories became occasions for overconfidence.

Perhaps, on the other hand, you feel discouraged that this devotional book hasn't made the difference that you hoped it would. Maybe you had high expectations that reading this work would give you the precise tools that you needed to finally kick your addictive habit. Maybe this book feels like one more thing you've tried that didn't work. But this book is simply a resource— a tool to help you think about yourself and about your God; it doesn't possess any power to change you. But God does have the power to change you.

Just because you didn't overcome your addictive habit in these thirty-one days doesn't mean that you can't. There are hundreds upon hundreds of people who have found freedom from their addictions. You are no exception (see 1 Cor. 10:13). The Scriptures themselves tell one story after another of people being taken from the grips of slavery into freedom—both literally and spiritually. Paul notes the freedom that the gospel of God gives us. He writes,

> Do you not know that the unrighteous will not inherit the kingdom of God? Do not be deceived: neither the sexually immoral, nor idolaters, nor adulterers, nor men who practice homosexuality, nor thieves, nor the greedy, nor drunkards, nor revilers, nor swindlers will inherit the kingdom of God. And such were some of you. But you were washed, you were sanctified, you were justified in the name of the Lord Jesus Christ and by the Spirit of our God. (1 Cor. 6:9–11)

Paul mentions several addictive habits in this statement (sexual sins and drunkenness most notably). Yet those who participated in these habits have been washed and sanctified. Paul says, "Such were some of you"—past tense. They aren't defined or owned by those sins anymore. The apostle has full confidence that *freedom is possible for the believer in Christ.*

The vital element in any transformation is Jesus Christ. If you've found that in the last thirty-one days you've had great success, don't become self-confident. Don't fall into that temptation that says, "You did it! You're past this!" Self-reliance and self-confidence are bound to lead you into sin again. Any success is the work of God's Spirit in you. Not only did you need him in order to get this far, you still need him. If, on the other hand, you find that the last thirty-one days haven't made a big impact on your life, turn afresh to Jesus. No book can produce change. Books are tools that God may use, but he is the one you truly need. God delights to help his children grow and change. If you don't feel like you are changing, don't give up! Run back to God.

This book has outlined what I believe to be a helpful approach to addictive habits. The Four R's, as I call them, can move individuals from the heart-level foundational issues to the practical life alterations that promote enduring change. We began with *responsibility*, understanding that we can't repent of what we don't own. We must own our choices, attitudes, thoughts, and desires, as these things contribute to the rise of an addictive habit and its exacerbation.

We moved to *relationship*, because change isn't simply about what we do. Many who have tried to quit an addiction know that on our own it's nearly impossible to make progress. We need God's grace and power to change us, and we need his church to help us stay the course. We can't overcome an addictive habit on our own. We need God's people to help us.

Restructuring our lives is vital for fighting against temptation and sin. We develop relapse-prevention plans, avoid temptation, and adapt to trials. We must augment our character and enjoy healthy amusements. We must also learn to be in awe of the beauty and glory of God.

Finally, we explored what it means to *remain* faithful in the long run. We are not done fighting an addictive habit just because the height of our troubles has passed. Remaining vigilant requires us to stay close to God and to godly people. Evaluating how we steward our whole lives for God's glory is an important element of maintaining success.

Responsibility. Relationships. Restructuring. Remaining. The Four R's are just one model, but they are a simple way of thinking about the nature of biblical change. If they are helpful for you, I encourage you to think through each element again. Think about where you are strongest and where you are weakest. Talk with a counselor or pastor who can help you develop a plan to grow in each element. Whatever you do, don't quit fighting. You can change, because God delights to change his people.

Acknowledgments

BOOKS ARE NEVER written alone, and there have been many hands involved in the writing of this book. While the content is my own, I could not have developed it in this format without the help of many people. Frank Tallerico was a constant source of wisdom and insight as I wrestled with ideas. Brad Hambrick helped to point me in the direction of important resources and sharpened my focus on some of the practical outworking of conceptual issues. Jonathan Holmes and Brad Bigney were kind enough to read drafts and give me feedback. Mark Shaw was a wonderful conversation partner, challenging me and giving me some different perspectives on certain points. My dear friend Tim Johnson, who leads our substance-abuse counseling table at Cornerstone, listened often and helped me to fine-tune my application questions. Finally, Deepak Reju has been a tremendous editor, offering me much patient guidance along the way.

Notes

Tips for Reading This Devotional

1. Jonathan Leeman, *Reverberation: How God's Word Brings Light, Freedom, and Action to His People* (Chicago: Moody, 2011), 19.

Introduction

1. See Kent Dunnington, *Addiction and Virtue: Beyond the Models of Disease and Choice* (Downers Grove, IL: IVP, 2011), esp. chaps. 1–3.

Day 1: Shame, Identity, and Change

1. Paul David Tripp, *Instruments in the Redeemer's Hands: People in Need of Change Helping People in Need of Change* (Phillipsburg, NJ: P&R, 2002), 260.

Day 3: You Become What You Worship

1. For more on this idea, see G. K. Beale, *We Become What We Worship: A Biblical Theology of Idolatry* (Downers Grove, IL: IVP, 2008), 122–23.

Day 5: Changing Kingdoms

1. Bob Dylan, "You Gotta Serve Somebody," recorded May 4, 1979, track 1 on *Slow Train Coming*, Columbia, 1979.

Day 7: Graves of Craving

1. Alternate ESV translation.

Day 24: Finding New Joy

1. Kristi Coulter, "Giving Up Alcohol Opened My Eyes to the Infuriating Truth about Why Women Drink," Quartz, August 21, 2016, https://qz.com/762868/giving-up-alcohol-opened-my-eyes -to-the-infuriating-truth-about-why-women-drink/. This quote and citation are not an endorsement of the overall article, which contains some very crass language and content!

Day 28: The Power of Gratitude

1. See Heath Lambert, *Finally Free: Fighting for Purity with the Power of Grace* (Grand Rapids: Zondervan, 2013), 26.

Day 31: The Grace That Endures

1. John Newton, "Amazing Grace," 1779.

Conclusion

1. This is a process called *stimulus generalization*, through which we learn to respond to a variety of stimuli with the same response: indulging in our addictive habit. So, if I drink to medicate bad feelings, I also learn to associate joy with drinking. Eventually I drink not just when I have a bad day, but when I want to have fun too.

Suggested Resources for Change

Bigney, Brad. *Gospel Treason: Betraying the Gospel with Hidden Idols*. Philipsburg, NJ: P&R, 2012. [Brad's book is a great introduction to the ways in which false worship often lies below the surface-level symptoms of our problems. Our life is about worship, and Brad demonstrates how false worship leads us into trouble.]

Fitzpatrick, Elyse. *Love to Eat, Hate to Eat: Breaking the Bondage of Destructive Eating Habits*. 1999. Reprint, Eugene, OR: Harvest House, 2004. [This is the only book I know of that thoroughly addresses an addiction to food from a Biblical perspective. And, fortunately, it is the only book you will need to read. Elyse outlines both a theological foundation and practical help for fighting against an obsession with food.]

Lambert, Heath. *Finally Free: Fighting for Purity with the Power of Grace*. Grand Rapids: Zondervan, 2013. [This is a short, but not a simplistic, book on fighting against sexual temptation and particularly pornography. Lambert is particularly good at highlighting the often overlooked tools that Christians can use in their fight against sexual sin.]

Shaw, Mark E. *Relapse: Biblical Prevention Strategies*. Bemidji, MN: Focus, 2011. [This is, in my opinion, hands down the best book on relapse prevention available. Not only does Mark give readers lots of great prevention strategies, but he gives them a theological framework in which to think about them rightly.]

Welch, Edward T. *Crossroads: A Step-by-Step Guide Away from Addiction*. Greensboro, NC: New Growth, 2008. [A very practical workbook for those struggling with substance abuse.]

Wilkerson, Mike. *Redemption: Freed by Jesus from the Idols We Worship and the Wounds We Carry*. Wheaton, IL: Crossway, 2011. [Using the story of the Exodus as a guide, Wilkerson walks readers through a journey to freedom from whatever addictions attempt to keep them in bondage. Full of great stories and illustrations of principles, this is a unique and valuable book for Christians.]

BIBLICAL
COUNSELING
COALITION

The Biblical Counseling Coalition (BCC) is passionate about enhancing and advancing biblical counseling globally. We accomplish this through broadcasting, connecting, and collaborating.

Broadcasting promotes gospel-centered biblical counseling ministries and resources to bring hope and healing to hurting people around the world. We promote biblical counseling in a number of ways: through our *15:14* podcast, website (biblicalcounselingcoalition.org), partner ministry, conference attendance, and personal relationships.

Connecting biblical counselors and biblical counseling ministries is a central component of the BCC. The BCC was founded by leaders in the biblical counseling movement who saw the need for and the power behind building a strong global network of biblical counselors. We introduce individuals and ministries to one another to establish gospel-centered relationships.

Collaboration is the natural outgrowth of our connecting efforts. We truly believe that biblical counselors and ministries can accomplish more by working together. The BCC Confessional Statement, which is a clear and comprehensive definition of biblical counseling, was created through the cooperative effort of over thirty leading biblical counselors. The BCC has also published a three-part series of multi-contributor works that bring theological wisdom and practical expertise to pastors, church leaders, counseling practitioners, and students. Each year we are able to facilitate the production of numerous resources, including books, articles, videos, audio resources, and a host of other helps for biblical counselors. Working together allows us to provide robust resources and develop best practices in biblical counseling so that we can hone the ministry of soul care in the church.

To learn more about the BCC, visit biblicalcounselingcoalition.org.